A Writer's Guide To Creative Blogging

A Writer's Guide To Creative Blogging

CREATE THE WRITER'S BLOG YOU'VE ALWAYS WANTED

Rebecca A Emrich and Paul Nieder

First Printing, 2015
For Love of Books
Kitchener Ontario

ISBN-13: 9780986600944
ISBN-10: 0986600946

To Our Loyal Website Readers,
and
Our Families

Table of Contents

A Start To Blogging

I HAD ALWAYS BEEN INTERESTED in the blogging world. I follow lots of blogs. I normally read them on my wife's iPad. I like blog posts because they allow me to connect to the writer in short bursts. The information is quick, and I can get the beginning, middle and end of the post in a few minutes.

Before coming to Living a Life of Writing, I had never blogged before. I enjoy having conversations about technical products in real life, and it was because of this I was able to join the tech world.

I met Rebecca in the context of her day job and was impressed with how friendly and down to earth she was. We didn't talk about blogging; instead we talked about our interests. I ended up sharing some stories about some current tech products that I would love to try out and some others that will be coming out later this year that sound interesting, too. It was because of this meeting that Rebecca asked me to write for her blog.

I was thrilled to be asked to blog on Living A Life of Writing. After a few days I settled in. This was not a blog that I was starting myself. This was a blog that had a core set of followers. This blog had been around for seven years and seen a number of guest bloggers come and go.

How was I going to stand out enough to be a regular? How was I going to stay?

When the resident "Tech Girl" moved on to book reviews I became the "Tech Guy". I had a fair amount of tech-type experience, but how would I translate that into writing blog posts that people would want to read?

I jotted all the ideas for posts I had down first; I wanted to get them out on paper so that I wouldn't forget any of them and so that I could form a plan.

The topic of my first post ended up being speech-to-text apps, and I decided that I wanted to review what was available for Apple's iPad. Then I set to work.

I downloaded lots of apps. I tried each one in both a quiet setting and in a mildly noisy setting. After I gathered my data and determined which one worked the best, I had had to turn that data into a post people would read.

I scribbled out the sentences that came to me. I added notes to my data and then began to type.

I was happy with the outcome. I made sure that Rebecca read it over before I posted it. It was a hit. People enjoyed it. I was nervous at first, but when people started commenting, and the comments were positive, I knew that I would fit right in.

The biggest surprise for me was how much time a seven hundred and fifty word post took to craft from start to finish.

Let's use the example of writing a review of several different apps that offer a particular "service". It can seem like an overwhelming task to find the apps, download them, try them out in different scenarios, and take notes as you go. By the time you finally get around to writing the piece, you have already done several hours of work. My first post took me close to five hours.

I can imagine that crafting a book review would take just as long, or longer, depending on how fast the reviewer reads, how long the book is, and then how much time the reviewer spends actually writing the post.

Spend the time on your posts. Short posts that don't really explore the subject matter and don't elaborate on the statements that you make aren't beneficial to your readers or for the site.

You are trying to convey information to someone. Telling them to try this and read that without telling them why is not helpful.

Creating an interesting one sided conversation is hard enough, but you also need to give the reader enough information so that they feel compelled to read the book, see the movie, or, in the case of tech reviews, buy the gadget or app that you recommend.

Plan what you are going to say. What is your opening statement? How will you entice the reader to continue on through your post and keep them there?

The quality of your opening statement is important. It sets up the reader for the subject matter to come, as well as encourages them to move forward. Beginning with a phrase like "This is a review about apps" is not a strong opening statement. It gives the reader no more information than that you are going to talk about the app, and that's it.

A stronger opening is, "I use speech-to-text apps every day to record my thoughts quickly".

This captures the reader's attention. In this case, the reader is quickly able to discern that the blog is a review and it will focus on speech to text apps, that these apps have a use in your everyday life, and that they make a job easier to finish quickly.

Once you have your opening statement, make a personal connection to the subject. Why do you use this product? Why did you read the book? Did it remind you of a personal story?

Since you are the storyteller, there has to be some *you* in it. I received this wonderful advice from a fellow writer on the Living a Life of Writing blog who did a post about review writing. Once I thought about it, I realized that she was right. How do you talk about how much you liked a product or service or recommend that someone to use it without including some description of your personal experience in the post?

With this all in mind, I started writing. I let ideas flow freely out of my mind. I added in my notes as I went, but I just wrote until I hit about five hundred words.

Next, I took some advice from Rebecca, and I walked away from my desk. I knew I needed at least two hundred and fifty more words to have a strong post. But I had exhausted my ideas and comments, so I took a break.

After ten minutes I came back to the piece and read it. I could see all my ideas and the data, but it didn't really flow. This is when I started the editing process. Editing doesn't always mean taking something out. In this case, editing not only helped me exceed the word count that I was striving to hit, but it also gave me the chance to better connect my thoughts.

My post started to take shape. Now it flowed. I just had to close the post, to wrap it up. I needed to write a summary of sorts that tied everything up and ended the piece.

Now that I'm a few months into writing blog posts, the posts themselves are now taking much less time to write than before. That being said, I am writing better pieces. I am more mature as a writer and have confidence in the opinions that I deliver.

When you are writing reviews, your opinion is the only one that matters in the piece. That's why people are reading it. They are looking to your wisdom to help them make a decision.

As for as tech reviews, if you go around asking other people what they thought about the item you are reviewing, that is a survey and not you forming your own opinion. You are likely to take those other people's opinions into consideration, and this will influence your original thoughts. Your reader is looking for your thoughts based on your experience evaluating a product.

Keep in mind that whatever subject you choose to review, you must have passion for it and good knowledge of that field.

It's also great to tell your audience, on the author biography section of the page or site, why you are qualified to give advice about your chosen topic, and why you have chosen to share your knowledge in the reviews.

Rebecca has been a successful author and blogger for the last seven years. Annabella has worked in the book industry for over ten years. Amanda has a social media background from her post-secondary education and has worked on the social media marketing campaigns for her current employer. I have over 30 years' experience with gadgets, computers, and console games as an end-user, and professionally as an IT product tester.

Once you have chosen your topic, check out what other blogs or websites that discuss similar subjects are doing. Look at their formats, what techniques do they use to keep the reader on the page and what makes people follow them.

Research is your friend. The blogosphere is an immense space. Be aware of what people are already reading, and consider carefully how your site can stand out.

Do you have the skills to create your own layout template to define the visual style of your blog?

Will you include videos, pictures, or guest bloggers?

Since the beginning of 2015, www.livingalifeofwriting.com has undertaken a lot of changes behind the scenes. We have taken two new people onboard, and formalized the list of responsibilities for each member of our team.

As you grow as a writer and blogger, your expectations of yourself and of your site should also grow.

If you no longer look for positive changes you could make, or for interesting content that you could add, your site could lose steam and fade away.

Another way to keep your blog going is posting fresh content regularly. At first you may not post every day.

Whether you have a busy schedule of work, school, your family, or all of the above, finding the time to fit everything in a day often gets complicated.

Managing your schedule is the key. On a weekly basis, I schedule time to work on my blog posts. I wake up an hour earlier than usual. I also try to find even thirty minutes during a quiet part of my day (when I'm not at my day job) to jot down my thoughts and check in on my social media accounts for responses to my blog posts. I have even made it a habit to check my smartphone for social media alerts and other messages that might inspire a new blog post during my break, at work.

Begin by setting goals for yourself. For example: if your goal is to write four blog posts a week for the first three weeks, write out all your engagements, appointments, work, and family obligations, and since you already know that a single blog post could take you a few hours from start to finish, you must now decide what days you will make the time to write them, and then on what days are the posts should go live on the Internet. Next, book your research and writing time.

Once you start finding the time to comfortably accommodate this number of posts in your schedule, you can think about increasing the number of blog posts per week. Are you able to post one per day?

As a writer and a blogger, I understand this seems a bit daunting and makes you want to stop before you even begin, but trust me, just write. Just sit down and write and don't let anything stop you from blogging.

Blogging and Making a Difference

THE ART OF WRITING ONLINE, known as blogging, is about making a difference in the lives of your readers. As a blog grows, so does the responsibility of the writer who first began to publish the blog. A reader comes to a blog with a specific need and the writer, in a short period of time must fulfil that need for that reader. Some readers come to a blog to find out more about a particular subject, and others come because they have forged a connection with the writer. A blog is a small place on the Internet, but it has the power change the outlook of each reader who visits it.

A blog, is in the strictest sense an online journal. A derivative from the name "web log", it serves as a platform for a person to put their thoughts out into the world. When blogging began, it was common for writers to use a more diary-like style of writing, where the focus is on self-reflection. The modern style focuses less on self-reflection and more on how the blogger can share personal experiences and knowledge from which the readers can learn.

The art of blogging grew and changed as more people felt the need to express themselves and have a positive impact on the lives of other writers. Your goal is to create great work that people want to read. Think about what you can give back to the online community with your blog. What's important is not how many hours you took to write a blog post, but how many writers you can touch with what you have to say. Set a goal for yourself of laying it all on the line and changing your readers' lives, or their writing lives, for the better.

Writers also need money. A blog can only make a difference in the lives of others if the writer is able to write a blog post without worrying about other parts of life affecting their work. If the writer is also publishing books, they have the added advantage of an additional stream of income and reinforcing the author's brand.

Some blogs will always be one person, writing on the blog or website, with that one person experiencing the many ups and downs a blog can have all alone. Other blogs have a group of people — bloggers, website designers, guest posters — who come and go and one or two writers who stay with the blog over the many years of its life. Some writers want quick riches and others want to make not only their dreams, but their readers' dreams a reality. Most bloggers eventually learn that they cannot stop writing and don't want to quit what they are doing; they love the process of blogging or at least having the ability to communicate with other readers and writers.

A part of writing some great blog posts and learning from more experienced writers and growing as a writer your-self, and then pushing against every painful limit you might have, and then, when it hurts too much to continue, you find that you are re-inventing yourself and pushing the new limit that your mind has created on your blog. Writing a blog is one of the most frustrating, emotional, passionate things you can do online because it requires time and energy to do anything of value — either financially or otherwise.

Some liken blogging to running a marathon without a defined finish line. Some blogs wither because the writers can't keep going, and some blogs re-invent themselves, and their writers create something far more powerful.

There are many blogs out there; some are brand new with excited writers and others are Internet marketers who either want to make money off of products they sell or want to showcase their technical skills to other Internet readers. There has been a virtual explosion of blogs since 2000, and the numbers will only increase as time goes on.

Some writers talk about achieve with their blogs. What makes a blog work is the connection between the people who write the blog and those who read them. There needs to be open communication between the two groups. A blog will only survive by re-inventing the blog's style occasionally and by fostering open communication between all parties.

Over time, every blog needs to be fixed up. Sometimes, it is because you've lost passion as a writer for the topic, and other times you need to bring in an additional person who will write posts for the blog and who will commit to improving the blog in other ways. Or, if you are a one-person blog, you must be willing to adapt the focus and structure of the blog if it is no longer resonating with your readers.

What About Blogging In general? Is There Something Every Writer Needs To Know?

WHERE YOU PUBLISH A BLOG is important. You have a lot of choices: Wordpress, Google's Blogger, Tumblr, and Wattpad are just a few of the great options available to you. They all do the same thing; they provide a writer with a platform. All of these places are built differently and they reach different audiences. They all have one thing in common: what you write and publish on any of them is called a "blog post". Readers have a lot of choice out there, and blogs like ProBlogger or the Huffington Post are the ones that writers can use as benchmark examples of successful blogs. Readers know that they can leave a blog at any time, but the blogger is committed to the blog, and for the long term. There is nothing wrong with thinking big, but if the majority of your posts are about 300 words long, you have a problem. Part of it is because a short post is now seen by readers as only a summary of your ideas and lacking support. For example, you might not think you have much to say about your favourite author, but the more you share of your personal opinions, the more likely a reader will be to find something in common with your message and leave a comment for you. You must write something a reader can connect with in the blog, and if they read one post for long enough, they might even find another one of your blog posts that they can also connect with along the way.

The best way to begin a blog post is to write down all your ideas about your subject freely as they come to you. Then, after you have all of that written, walk away from it for a while. If you're working on a computer, minimize the window you are in. You need some time away from what you've just composed. Give yourself about 20 minutes, and relax; read some other blog posts or a book. Do something to get away from your blog — or at least to get away from this particular post. Now go back and look at your creation. Is it helpful? Is it worth five minutes of your readers' time? Would you take time read it?

If you answered no to any of these questions, then it's not a good post — yet.

For a blog just starting out, you want your readers to stay on a blog post for about 30 seconds to a minute. Most readers, if they do not like the blog will leave in less time than that. Posting a longer piece means a reader will likely have to scroll down and will see links to additional relevant posts and links sites along the side of the page as they go. Including links to other posts helps a blog because if the blog now has an interested reader, he or she will more likely click on that link to see what else the authors have written or recommended.

But there is hope for this post; there is always time to fix it before it's published!

The one question that always needs to be answered with a "yes" is: Is it worth your readers' time to read the post? If you can't answer this one positively, even after you've done your editing, do not publish it yet. If you have something emotional to say and you don't feel that you can edit it yourself, have someone else look at it. This doesn't mean that your ideas aren't good enough to share with your readers; it simply means that you care enough to go back and reanalyze and rework the way you're sharing them. Your writing needs to be moving, and it needs to articulately communicate what you want the reader to understand. This doesn't mean you shouldn't use humour or use satire to illustrate your ideas, but it does mean you need to think carefully about how your reader will receive your writing and if those tools are appropriate for this piece of work. You might like music by the band called Genesis, but knowing that several of your readers don't can make a difference in the way you share that information with your readers. Saying, generally, that you like music and that you listen to it while writing is one thing, but take the specifics more slowly, otherwise some of your readers won't be able to follow you.

Here is an example: The introductory sentence, "The progressive rock band, Genesis, who were led by drummer Phil Collins..." helps you set the tone for the post. People can readily identify the person whom you are referring to. If you instead say, "Phil Collins is one of the best drummers alive," and you don't back up your opinion with logical arguments, a lot readers won't understand where the statement is coming from, and they will find it hard to make a connection with you. Do not assume that your readers will always agree with your opinions, but sometimes that disagreement works well, too, as a conversation-starter in the comments. Someone might even say, "This drummer is the best because..." and the next person could chime in, "Oh! You're right; that drummer is good, but you should all look out for this new amazing person who is just breaking onto the scene!" The truth is, some readers are only looking for basic information, and others are happy to read more.

The trick is to satisfy both audiences. Your personal view counts, but you need to make sure you communicate it carefully to your blog readers. And if you do it well, your readers will leave knowing you cared enough to spend time learning about your chosen topic and sharing both the facts you learned and the opinions that you formed in your post.

"Would I want to read this?" is a good question to ask yourself before you publish a post. If you are confused by the way you've expressed an idea after you've left your post alone for a while, it's not a good idea to publish it until you've done more editing. Perhaps a particular sentence just needs to be moved to another part of the post, or cutting it out and adding some interesting bits of trivia. Over the years blogging and editing has become a lot easier thanks to advances in technology, but the goal of expressing oneself well remains constant.

Readers care about how you feel about a particular topic or the challenges you face when writing and how you overcome them. A personal story doesn't need to go into great graphic detail, but it should offer some examples from personal experience and advice that the readers can use to help themselves through similar circumstances.

A blog post is not your online soap box, either. It should be a place where you share information about topics that help or interest your readers. You can discuss and add a link to your book, if you have one, but if you continuously advertise your book to your readers, they will tune you out. People will look for a blog post for different reasons. Offer your own experiences and examples to help them answer the questions that they came with, and also share any other relevant Internet links that you found helpful when that same question arose for you.

A blog is a place where readers and writers can connect and be inspired by the blog posts create. The comments section of a blog post is equally important as the post itself. A blog should inspire comments from its audience, and as the writer of that post, you should also actively respond to comments and questions from your readers to help you establish a relationship with them. Some of the best posts come about because a writer and reader have "hashed out" parts of a new blog post in the comments of a previous one. The more good-quality comments a post generates, the better the chances are your post will be well received by the greater writing community.

Readers might also recognize you from comments that you leave on other websites, and they appreciate that you have taken time and effort to write and respond to their words. While most comments are constructive and valuable, there are comments that can, and often should, be deleted designated as spam.

By definition, spam is a message that contains a link to online content that the reader does not intend to see. Most often, spam messages link to adult-content websites, "get rich quick" schemes, pharmaceutical sellers and other sites that target unsuspecting internet users with the intent of fraudulently obtaining money or personal information. Many writers, in an effort to avoid spam comments, make a request not to add links to other websites in the comments. Most people who read a blog are not spammers, so carefully looking at the types of comments with links in them can let a blogger know if they have someone who is abusing the system to direct more traffic to their own blogs. Bloggers can often identify auto-generated spam by looking for a lack of directly relevant communication in the comment leaver's part. "This was a great article; here is my website" is common enough spam text that the automatic detection systems on most blogging platforms will successfully identify it as such and put it into the spam box for the writer to moderate. Others are a bit more subtle; these ones mention their websites, but in a more roundabout way, as in, "I once wrote an article about this here [linked]," but the blogger has never seen the commenter before, and they leave no other details about the linked article or their opinions on the subject at hand.

Spam comments, by their very nature, are harder to identify when one is still new at blogging. Another clue to look for is the URL they may give in addition to their names. Some spam bots write what seems to be an insightful comment but the link provided with the commenter's name is where the click-bait is hidden.

It is the blog administrator's job to keep everyone safe. This job includes verifying the links that they use in the body of each post.

Most readers see value in a link that serves as a doorway to some other relevant or related web page. Some bloggers post links between their own related blog posts, and others will post a link to their book's page on Amazon.com. This is common and accepted practice. Be sure that, if you post links to other bloggers' writing sites, you go visit those sites regularly and make sure they are still live because blogs tend not to run for very long unless there is a dedicated blogger or writer driving them. Relevant links to articles on bigger sites such as the Huffington Post or other reputable online sites are also valuable.

Forging solid lines of communication and building good relationships with your readers is helpful. A reader with whom you have a good relationship is more likely to feel comfortable letting you know that she couldn't follow a link, and if you create a "Contact Us' page, other less-familiar readers will feel welcome to send an email to the blog owners so that errors or broken links can be fixed up in a timely manner. Sometimes, spam is hard to find and links break or go dormant, and if there isn't a person making certain things are running smoothly on a blog, things can fall apart.

Readers of a good informational blog expect content that has substance. They want to be able to relate to the challenges a writer has, but if the writer is sharing a negative experience, readers also likely want to see how the writer turned that negative situation into a positive one.

A Basic Primer to Blogs and Blog Posts

A LOT OF NEW WRITERS misjudge how long a post they should write. If the blog post generates comments like, "The post is short," it means the post has fallen below the magic number of 300 words, and the commenter believes that you have more good information to share. Occasionally, posts will be longer than 500 words, and these are more often personal experience posts, or more detailed "how-to" posts, and there will be some shorter posts published in between. Readers understand that sometimes you will have more or less to say based on your choice of topic.

The first thing a writer needs to know is that a good blog post, like beauty, is in the eye of the reader. Barring a nasty cause of writer's block, writing and publishing a blog post is a simple thing to do. Most of the popular platforms offer a very familiar word-processor-style interface. You write a few lines, and you add a picture or two, and you hit publish. Possibly if you have the time and the knowledge you can add a link to a relevant video or create one yourself. Blogging is, at its core, as simple as writing a not-so-personal journal. It gives the writer the opportunity to share ideas and information with potential readers.

However, to build a successful writing blog, you need to have more than just a post. You need to understand what a "good" blog post should look like.

Experienced bloggers suggest writing about 300 to 500 words per blog post, and the more helpful the content in it is, the more likely your readers will stay and read to the end. If you are creating a blog about writing, this is the absolute minimum number of words per post that you should write. Luckily, the subject of "writing" offers a nearly endless source of material.

At the time when Living a Life of Writing first began in 2008 it was common for serious blog writers to publish three or four blog posts of about 100 words each per day. By the time our blog was a year old, this idea fell out of fashion. It took more than just posting random ideas every day to keep the reader coming back to your blog. In my case, my readers didn't concern themselves with how many words a day I wrote, but they were interested in my thought process when I was editing, and what tools I used to make the process of writing and editing easier. Telling the reader that I could proofread my work by using spell check meant little unless I also explained which particular software program I used for checking spelling and grammar.

The goal of a writing blog, and the posts within, was to find ways to help people with your writing. The more powerful your message the more likely your readers are to leave comments on your blog posts, stay on your blog and read other linked posts within your site, and to also mention your blog on other writing web sites and social networking sites.

The last three paragraphs represent the approximate length of a standard blog post. It is a bit short, and isn't formatted the way a blog post would be, which is to say the paragraphs are a bit long and the information isn't supported with links or pictures.

Your readers are looking for something of value in your blog post. The post should be a balance between personal experiences and how to do something as it relates to your writing. Your writing blog ought to touch on how to write and what software you use, but also what methods of writing you choose for each particular medium. One writer might share that they begin with pen and paper and then move to a computer whereas another will go directly to the keyboard. You can write about your favourite writing software, and add a personal touch by saying you journal with pen and paper. The more often that readers find you to be a credible resource to draw on, the more likely they will be to see your blog as being more than a frivolous social media update. If you don't establish yourself as a source of interesting and useful information, you are in trouble.

Following the 300-500 word count guideline after about the tenth blog post will help to keep the attention of your readers. Most bloggers would like their readers to stay on a blog post for about 30 seconds to a minute. Most readers, if they do not like the blog will leave in less time than that. Posting a longer piece means a reader will likely have to scroll down and will see links to additional relevant posts and links sites along the side of the page as they go. Including links to other posts helps a blog because if the blog now has an interested reader, he or she will more likely click on that link to see what else the authors have written or recommended.

Blogging is not for the faint of heart. Writing a 500-word blog post might seem daunting to a blogger who has other daily commitments, but as time goes on and writing becomes part of your routine, it is time to consider writing longer blog posts. Most professional bloggers write a minimum of 700 words per post.

Evolution of blogging and search engines

A BLOG CAN GROW AND change over many years, and it requires constant editing. Going back to the beginning of a blog and looking over each individual post to see that they all still fit well with the style of the blog as a whole, is a smart idea. Part of this is because of your readers' natural curiosity to see how you have grown as a writer, and others might come across your older articles by way of search engine results.

The evolution of major Internet search engines changed the blogosphere dramatically. When Blogger.com, one of the first blog publishing platforms, launched in 1999, there were not a lot of dedicated bloggers, but by the time the company was bought by Google in 2003, the Internet had evolved. Google was founded in 1998, although the development of its search engine algorithms began in 1996. Google's takeover of Blogger made it a strong competitor in the blogging market.

And a lot changed two years later with the rise of WordPress and the option to make a blog a website as well. When this happened, a shorter blog post was ranked lower by the search engines, and dismissed as less valuable by other bloggers. Professional writers make money with their writing, and for many, placing sponsored advertising links next to their content became an accepted way to generate revenue. Because these ads are chosen by a computer program, based on key words and phrases in the post, the accepted blog standard of many short posts per day changed. A blog that showcases great content in the eyes of readers and other writers isn't evaluated by search engines in the same way. While the search engines themselves do not have relationships with bloggers, bloggers have to communicate with them to build new relationships with their readers.

To Google, a blog title is everything, but a writer shouldn't spend hours trying to guess what will attract the attention of a reader. Some "how-to" posts rank better when linked with a personal story blog post. Bloggers started noticing an increase in the number of visits to a page if a writer on a larger writing blog wrote a how to post after they had written a personal story post. That increase in numbers and the subsequent discussion about the relationship between that increase and the types of posts sparked discussion in blog post comments and in other online forums. Writers could say, "This was my personal experience, but here are my numbers so you can look them over and decide for yourself."

Book Review Blog Posts

ON LIVING A LIFE OF Writing we do a lot of book review posts. Following the basic minimum blog post word count, these are some of the things needed for a successful book review post.

A book review blog post, for example, needs to contain at least two things: the book's title and its author. Your review should include a short description of the book's theme and plot, and then you should go into more detail about what you thought of the book and, perhaps, how it made you feel, if it evoked strong emotions. Some book review blogs include a video of the reviewer's reaction to a particular book. So famous was the toss into the air and dancing for joy reaction to a book- the review post was the talk of many bloggers for a long while. If you write a more personal note blog, make sure if you think your opinion might be controversial, write your ideas out and then leave them alone for a while. Look over and edit your words again before publishing them be confident that you believe in your words and that you've phrased your ideas as best you can, and then let the chips fall where they may. You have no control over your readers' reactions, but if you present good supporting information, you may win some of them over.

What A Blog Needs to Be a Success

NEVER ASSUME THAT YOUR BLOG will be an overnight success. Most professional bloggers I've consulted with say it takes about five to six years to build consistent levels of traffic, attract more comments, and to generate consistent income. This happens only after they have done three things: accepted the necessity of reinvention, adopting a consistent and accessible writing style, and making a connection with their readers. Writers who attract over a million views per year do so because of the relationships they have developed with others. They focused on their blogs. And they learned from mistakes that they made with other blogs before they found "it" with this blog. Some writers give up in frustration because of the sheer amount of *time* it takes to write and publish posts and to do everything else that makes a blog successful.

To attract more traffic you have to stand out from the crowd. Your writing blog is one in several million and yours has to be found by other writers who want to do exactly the same thing. You will face a lot of challenges along the way in this crowded market space. Once you have momentum, you will have the chance to make a difference in the writing community.

Blogging is not for the faint of heart. Writing a 500-word blog post might seem daunting to a blogger who has other daily commitments, but as time goes on and writing becomes part of your routine, it is time to consider writing longer blog posts. Most professional bloggers write a minimum of 700 words per post.

If the subject of a blog post is helpful to your readers, and it's also a topic that you are passionate about, that will shine through in your writing and editing, and it will be a good blog post. Good titles for your posts, and a consistent following of reader's area great, but photos, and word of mouth promotion will help you even more. A professional writer will use a blog differently than a company that is focused on serving customers and making money.

Citizen journalism will always exist, and many blogs on the web are no longer active – meaning that the writer hasn't updated or posted to the blog for more than a year. Some sources like, problogger.net, believe this number to be as high as 65 percent, but don't concern yourself with becoming part of that statistic; instead strive to create a professional and interesting blog.

Every blog has the potential to earn money if the writer dedicates time and energy to it. Most writers are looking for financial freedom so that they only have to write for possibly four to six hours a week. However, the most successful writers write a lot. The best writers have published many books for readers to choose from. The same holds true when a writer has more than one project on the go, especially a writing blog which depends so heavily on strong relationships between the writer and readers. It is unwise to expect that you will earn much more than one hundred dollars for the first six months of a blog's life, because you won't have the traffic like other larger blogs will have. It is far more common for a writer to give up and quit before they begin earning the money they hope for.

Once a blogger decides that it is time to make their blog more professional in both the writing and the blog's design, often an increase in income will follow. A blog needs to attract at least 500 views per day to earn steady income for the blogger who is writing about a topic on the Internet where the competition is lower. In the case of a fiercely competitive market, like the topic of writing, a blogger should aim for double or triple this number. The payout threshold for Google, for example, is 100 US dollars, 100 British pounds, 100 Euros, or the equivalent in the local currency. A blog about writing needs to get close to 20,000 or more views per month to generate a good level of income from this affiliate program. For a blog about making money, or about blogging, it's reasonable to suggest that 40,000 views per month will earn them some healthy income. The market for these topics is very saturated, so there is less competition between advertisers for readers' attention, and therefore the blogger receives less income per visit to her blog.

Bloggers will also use Amazon to research and recommend books. This is helpful to the blog's readers because they can see what the writer enjoyed reading and what they didn't. Recommendations of books, products, or services by a reputable blogger, which include personal experiences, often help readers make decisions about whether to try or to buy that same item for themselves.

Some of the best blogs include pictures or videos that support the point of view that the blogger is presenting. Because readers are looking for as many ways to connect with the writer as possible, it's not enough anymore to have only plain text in your blog posts. While each blog post still needs to meet the 300 word count threshold, adding pictures, and links can help a blog convey the writer's ideas better to the reader.

Your blog needs to stand out in the crowd. If your blog is simply a commentary on your writing life and nothing more, then it's going to stay in the shadows and won't make a difference in the lives of readers and other writers. It takes courage and the willingness to learn from constructive criticism for you to grow as a blogger. If a blog's information is helpful, but only in the most recent period of time, go back and refresh what was written before. Current information and improved style will make the ideas you want to continue to share more accessible and attractive to your audience. A blog is a changeable thing. It is an extension of the writer, and a blog won't change as long as the writer isn't willing to evolve and grow personally for the sake of the blog.

Blogging is Being Human, and Sharing Experiences

A BLOG ISN'T RUN BY itself; humans run a blog. The volume of forgotten or retired blogs reflects this reality. A person must have the passion and the desire to change a blog for the better. Some of the most prolific writers have said that their blogs didn't connect with their readers until they challenged themselves to be more open about what they most feared. Often, we are afraid of criticism because criticism begets change, and that can be scary. No writer likes to hear that their blog has problems, just as no person likes to hear that they have to change something about their lifestyle for the benefit of heath, or that they aren't making the impact on the world that they thought they were.

A writer needs to make changes to their blog when what they once did doesn't work anymore. To simply keep on writing about complicated book spines, or how exhausting it can be to write a blog, or how hard it is to publish a book and maintain a decent work/life balance at the same time, turns very quickly into an endless-sounding "poor me writer" broken record. The best blogs change, and the best writers evolve, but this happens only when writers challenge themselves to do so.

One of the greatest powers a writer has is the power of creativity. Writers are often perceived by the outside world to be wildly creative people, but this isn't always the case. Many writers are normal, organized, goal oriented people who are able to take an idea a spin it around and expand on it. Many successful writers have faced setbacks in their lives and careers, some of which are the stuff of legend, and others just found their groove later in life. There are very few people who say that they achieved instant success. There are even fewer who don't have a strong emotional support system, and some just had a lightning strike of good luck before they found their groove.

A writer is human, and humans need to face challenges before they can change for the better. A writer must challenge himself to explore the depth and breadth of the emotional scale most people don't want to contemplate. For some people, writing is the only thing that kept them going during hard times. By writing a journal, they were able to both internalize and externalize their pain to others as they worked through some of those challenges. Writers seem to be more willing to face their many demons than other people. This does not mean that the writer rarely thinks positive thoughts, but rather the writer turns a naturally negative situation into a blog post that serves to be inspirational to others.

The pain and joys of life are best described by a writer who has felt them. The challenges they were able to face and learn from make them more interesting writers. Better writers write better blogs. A blog, much like a private personal journal, offers the writer an opportunity to stop her thoughts from running wild through her head and put them into a concrete form. It provides her with a lens through which to analyze those thoughts better. Blogging helps a writer mature and grow personally, as well, because real life is not without pain and learning.

Some of the best writers don't share every detail of their lives, but they are willing to share one or two on their blog to help other writers understand the ideas that they wish to share. If a writer doesn't or feels he can't share personal stories, perhaps because he fears receiving a negative response from his readers, they may not fully understand what writer is trying to convey. A more

personal post will stand the test of time and will rein-
force the idea that a negative situation, which the writer
faced didn't stop them from continuing on their writing
journey.

Sometimes, though, a writer can face too many challenges in her life for her creative mind to handle, and she
should ask the people around her to support her. Most
writers are naturally positive people, and they seem to
deal well with life's ups and downs as they develop. Some
writers unintentionally add to their own challenges, but
overcoming those challenges makes them and their writing better for it. A blog is a much more open journal, and
while some writers choose to write both a physical journal
and a blog, it is more common for younger writers to use
at least one blog as their personal journal online.

A public blog involves the writer being willing to explore her own limits of endurance and communication
style. It is not unusual for a writer to schedule specific
times for writing blog posts, so that her readers can come
to expect a post at a specific time during the day. Other
writers, when they discover that they have a free block of
time, set aside distractions such as phones and email, and
they just sit and write. Either method gives the writer
time to reflect, to write and to edit that particular piece,
and also to reflect on writing in general.

Writing is not a selfish endeavour. Once something is published it is no longer exclusively the writer's own.

Although some bloggers are comfortable with sharing all of their demons, others are not. Many blogger-writers take their cue from the more famous writers of the 20th century; Ernest Hemingway, F. Scott Fitzgerald, and C. S. Lewis are among famous writers who hid their demons so well that they were only discovered after their deaths.

J. R. R. Tolkien is one of the most popular fantasy writers, and he is known as the grandfather of the fantasy genre. He was a soldier, commissioned as a Second Lieutenant, in the First World War, and he fought in the battle of the Somme. When readers commented on the parallels of his books to the events of the Second World War, he often replied that they must know their history of war very well.

He took time to translate Beowulf as well, and this, along with his interest in cultural and literary studies of Old English and German, helped to make him into a master at the fantasy genre. He drew on this passion as well as his first-hand knowledge of war and his feelings about it to create some of the best-known and emulated battle scenes in fantasy and in fiction.

Readers relate well to him, not necessarily because of his writing style, but because of how carefully he worked his own experiences of war and the deaths of many beloved friends into his writing. He could very well have died during the war, and his seeming awareness of this is reflected in his writing. It stands out to many people who read his novels and wonder how much the life he led influenced his writing.

Tolkien was also not the only writer to use his personal experiences to shape his writing. Tolkien not only influenced his writing contemporaries and his readers, but he influenced countless other writers who came after him. *The Inheritance Cycle* by Christopher Paolini is strongly influenced by Tolkien and his Nordic Mythology. Other authors such as Terry Brooks were so heavily influenced by the *Lord of the Rings* series that his works, specifically *The Sword of Shannara,* are considered to be homages to Tolkien's writing. Tolkien focused on his own experiences to great effect, and he used those challenges and experiences to create powerful books, whereas Brooks and Paolini did not directly face the horror of war, and they could only draw on historical writings and their own imagination for their stories.

A writer can share with words, descriptive imagery, and with illustrations and photographic images what he loves and what he cares about. This can make a blog better. The life experience of a more mature writer can influence how a reader responds to a blog. The same holds true with how a blog is perceived by a reader at first glance. A blog can only take off and soar when the writer is willing to be open to both personal and professional growth. People naturally want to hear stories that describe a positive outcome rising from a negative situation. The more frequently a blog can offer this to its readers the more likely it is that the blog will be successful.

A writer, like a blog, needs time to grow. It's not only important to improve what you say but also how you say it. The style a writer uses to share ideas will change over time. The strong technical and emotional foundations of a writer help make growth possible. The writer's thoroughness of preparation and the set of challenges that she faces in her life and writing will naturally alter the way she observes the world around her.

The power and passion for writing can wax and wane each day. There will be days when there are too many commitments, and take comfort in the fact that this happens to everyone. Commitments, forgotten or not, come at inopportune times for every person. However, these can affect a writer differently than other people because many writers feel they must say yes to almost anything they are asked to do. Writing for a living is, by nature, a hard road to travel, and the process by which a writer decides what he can, and conversely can't, take on is vital to their growth as a writer, and to their personal wellbeing. Saying yes any time that someone offers work for money is not the answer.

Without taking time and energy to reflect on their writing and blogs, a writer will not develop and mature, and she might fall back into bad habits, such as not posting on a regular basis, which when they were less known, or were younger, worked well for them, but does not work now. Understanding and overcoming their limitations, and balancing their work and life is the only way for a writer to continue to survive and thrive. A balanced, emotionally mature writer intentionally looks at what they do, and pauses and reflects. In the context of blogging, this might not be the simplest thing to do.

While a writing blog makes one a part of the greater blogging community, the blogosphere, there is something special about each writer.

Does A Writer Need to Change?

WRITERS NEED TO CHANGE, OR mature, to build a better blog. Because the act of blogging is done by one writer, it is often harder to change how you write without being inspired by a negative experience. Readers of a blog cannot force a writer to change their style or even how they see their writing. Readers have influence on blogs they read, but a reader of a blog cannot 'make' a writer want to improve a blog in ways they want them to do, it is up to the writer to reflect, accept and improve to grow a blog each day. If the concept of change is viewed positively by the writer, the more likely he will challenge their writing limits and make needed changes their readers have suggested.

Forcing big change on anyone will likely have negative consequences. It can erode the spirit of the writer, and it will diminish the enthusiasm for writing a blog, or writing in general. A writer should find confidence in another person or reader who helps to improve a blog with constructive critiques and praise when needed. This will in turn help the writer have a sharper vision of what he wants his blog to become. If a writer faces too much criticism in the beginning of a blogging career, there is more of a chance that he will not continue. Not enough suggestions for improvement, and the career they envisioned for themselves will fail when true, constructive comments happen later on in his blogging career.

A well-balanced blog has one or two people working together and allows both of them to reflect and develop a plan for rebuilding a blog that has stopped growing. Keep lines of communication open, and build trust. Each writer should cultivate a more powerful and healthy image of himself. This can't be forced, and if it is, each side will feel resentment. The more experiences a writer has to reflect on and to build from the more they will learn and grow.

Communication is a skill that a writer can improve with ease. A blog is a changing Internet creation, and bloggers need to strive to have a blog that sees readers and other bloggers as a part of their team.

Writing as a Team Sport

IF YOUR BLOG HAS MORE than one writer, it's especially important to keep the lines of communication open between all
the team members. It is more important if the team is not
in the same city or if there are great differences in personal-
ity. No two writers write the same way, and it shouldn't be
expected that all the writers keep to the same blog post style
or topic. The writers should share a common vision for the
direction of the blog. There should be a leader, but this person does not need to be the one who created the blog or the
one who writes he most posts, it should be the one who can
earn and keep the respect and the commitment of the other
writers. There should be some form of regularly scheduled
group meeting where concerns and new topics can be raised
and discussed, and where everyone participates.

Having more than one writer contributing to a blog
means that the ground rules you set for your team must

be maintained. Regularly discuss, as a group, what works well and what doesn't. A blog will survive only as long as all team members work together.

Following a schedule helps too. Loyal readers will learn quickly if the blog writers follow a pattern for posting; for example, one writer will always post something on a Tuesday, and another will post once a month on a Friday, and the last one posts every second week on a Monday. As a team, a linking idea or shared theme should be adopted. The blog posts should also have links between team members' posts on each blog so a loyal reader of one writer can find out more from another.

Keeping an open line of communication between team members can sometimes prove difficult, and a complete lack of communication will certainly cause problems. To help prevent some conflicts, establish very clearly who is responsible for doing what and when. If only one writer actively promotes the blog on social media networks, but the rest do not, even though they have promised to do so, this can create a tension point. Scheduling monthly, or even weekly meeting sessions — sometimes one to one or sometimes as a whole group — will help make sure every writer, and editor, and blog designer understands the common goals and individual responsibilities for the given period. It is important for each person to be held accountable for his or her writing. If one writer says she will post her writing on a Tuesday, and she does not, have a designated team member speak with her to find out why.

Why an Editor is Important

EDITORS ARE IMPORTANT, BUT FINDING yourself working with a wrong editor who pushes you too hard or doesn't push hard enough will feel just as much like a forced change as one that comes from blog visitors' comments, well-meaning acquaintances, non-writers, or new readers. Editors are a part of your writing team. The power behind a blog is its inherent adaptability, and the heart and foundation of a writer needs to be open change as a writer needs to be result of open communication and reflection. 'Writing it out' is good advice if the person doing so has the time and energy to create one more thing in an effort to improve.

A good editor will work with you and with your writing. While the book that you are working shares a lot about how you as a person and writer view the world, it also creates a focus for your problems as well. No writer is perfect, and most drafts go through many revisions before they get published in print. Unfortunately, this isn't the case with a blog. A lot of writers will admit, on occasion, to just publishing a blog post right then and there because they were pressed for time and wanted a post to be up and done. The problem with this scenario, if it happens too often, is that the writer becomes too comfortable and complacent how much editing they feel that they need to do, and then they will be less likely to take the much more painful step in editing when they are writing for publishing beyond the blog.

An editor who works closely with a blogger needs to look at the blog objectively and carefully before they begin to 'rip up' a poorly managed blog. The editor must be honest and open with the writer, but he must also be patient and willing to allow the improvement to take place over a period of time. Some blog will only become successful once the main blogger receives editing help. Part of the goal is to encourage the writer to better explain the details of their ideas to the editor (and eventually to the readers), and the other part is to have the editor constructively and clearly state what is and is not working on a blog. The editor must walk a fine line so as not to be mean and make the writer feel defensive about her work, but rather the editor must challenge her to push her limits. Some writers will not grow and improve without encouragement from a powerful editor. While there are times when an editor can and should back down, most of the time, if there is good and open communication between editor and blogger, the writer's work will begin to shine.

On a more personal note, Living a Life of Writing didn't hit its stride until several of the authors took a chance at being more open to the readership about their challenges, joys, and life in general. While it was a very emotionally charged choice, it forced them all to use real life challenges and relationships to connect with their readers. The readers responded, and while some reacted with unkind words, most respondents were open about their own feelings and delighted with the changes. This encouraged the authors to continue writing about their personal journeys through life, and the evolution was not forced, but it was planned and enjoyed by both blog writers and readers a like.

There was no particular force behind this change in direction; rather, it came about because of open lines of communication, and learning how to say what we wanted to say and using those words to move the blog in a positive direction. Most writers instinctively know that they need to say something to another writer to make it better, others know it's a part of building an audience who wants to go and read your blogs. A blog, no matter how dynamic needs to have an intelligent and wise blogger at the helm, and not one who focuses on the one way, or the one means they don't need to change.

We were encouraged to change the blog, and we found to our delight the ability to see the negatives in the light of how a reader sees our writing was the catalyst for a natural progression in our daily blog posts. It helped us focus on the most needed upgrades right away. From deleting older, and broken links to adding correct images and more content, it improved the overall reading experience for our readers.

Encouragement is an illusion as well, since more often than not, unless there is a long time established writing connection where the reader and writer have some form of relationship and can understand what the other person might be saying minus eye contact and body language, the writer might think someone is being encouraging when the relativity is the exact opposite. Sometimes it is best to question rather than assume. Some people are by nature not encouragers, and will tell it like it is, others are more of the true encouragers and a blog writer can take everything at face value- if they know the person. Some however, use a blog platform to make it look as if they encouraging the blogger, only to have them figure out it is a backhanded compliment since the maxi with these commentators is "don't say anything mean, but it's okay to be a bit mean later on." These are the readers a blog writer needs to be aware of, for they are the ones who hold the most truth.

Finding out what works with comments and negative feedback is one thing, using it to improve a blog is another. A backhanded compliment is one of the best ways to learn about editing since it makes bloggers think what should be better on a blog for their readers. If a person- or several people- consistently say this blog post is good, but if you go back far enough on the blog itself this isn't, then there is a problem with the fundamental overview of the blog. A person who is more inclined towards numbers and number crunching might not see what a reader sees, but can take an analysis of the situation and upgrade as needed.

Blogs Writers and Growth

CAN YOUR BLOG OR WEBSITE grow if you add other bloggers?

Livingalifeofwriting.com is a community. As a group of writers, we rely on each other for fresh posts every day. We want to be sure that each person's content mixes well with the others, and so we meet regularly to discuss blog matters.

To take a blog and make it into a business you need a solid team.

The team's dynamic is essential to growing as a business. Great teamwork means more ideas are brought forward, fresh views are welcome, and, ultimately, more work gets done.

Shortly after I joined the team we were starting to look at roles in the leadership capacity. My strength is not numbers, so when Annabella was chosen for the role of CFO (Chief Financial Officer), I was not heart broken. Rebecca was chosen for the role of CEO (Chief Executive Officer) because she is the driving force and creator of our two main websites. Amanda is a natural COO (Chief Operating Officer) because she is very detail-oriented and has a great sense of organization, so when she was chosen for that position, I congratulated her. But where did that leave me?

And I was named President. I'm not even President of my house; my wife takes that role. Since I like to continue to eat well, I will never complain about that. She is a valuable person in my life.

As President at Living A Life Inc. I am responsible for running the meetings that we have, I oversee my social media accounts, I am responsible for overseeing the video game blog, www.livingalifeofgaming.com which launched at the end of April, and I write reviews and posts for the multiple blogs within our network of sites. My teammates keep me busy and inspired.

I feel very positive about the part that I play for the blog. My writing style is different from the others who write for this blog. If you read a post and don't look at the name, you would likely be able to identify its author from the tone and writing style.

As one novice blogger to another, the best piece of advice that I can give is to keep writing. Maybe you are not ready to host a blog or site on your own yet; however, keep writing your thoughts down. Write practice articles, and have a trusted friend read them. Only blog when you are ready. There are thousands of blogs that don't make it. They fizzle out because the writer gets bored or just doesn't care about it anymore. I have meet all of these types' people with blogs. I want to ask them why they gave up. Why didn't they bring a friend on board to lighten the workload so that the blog — something that they did once enjoy — can continue on?

It takes a support system to grow a blog to the level that livingalifeofwriting.com has achieved today. That might be one of the biggest things that I have learned over the course of this process. If your team's members all have the same vision for the project, and they are working together towards the same goals, then you will succeed.

Because of all the group meetings, the help from my fellow blog-mates and lots of reading how-to guides, I have been able to build a solid foundation to work from. Anyone can start a blog; one just has to know what one wants to write about and set concrete expectations and tangible goals.

I have already said blogs take time. A lot of time. But I have solely focused on the site and writing.

What about all the other work for your blog that keeps people coming back?

It's not enough to blog and hope people would read it. You have to make sure people see it. Twitter, Facebook, Google+ and LinkedIn are all sites to grow your network. I tend to spend about an hour to an hour and a half every day just on social media. Every day I'm posting my own and my fellow bloggers blog posts to Twitter, Facebook and Google+ and making connections through LinkedIn globally, to build my network.

Your network of people will only grow if you put time in. I read all my Twitter messages and respond. I respond to all comments that are posted on my blog posts. I'm actually a little sad when there's no comments. I thrive on them.

I listen to my reader's feedback. If they want to hear about certain products, I will review them. They want to know more about something that I review, I will show them how to find it.

On Twitter, Facebook and Google+, I share other people's work (pictures, quotes and promos for their own books) on my feeds. This way when this book is launched or when something big happens on the site, then I know people will retweet or post my work. I scratch their back, they scratch mine.

When it comes to LinkedIn, do not only look for people local to you or doing the same thing. It's fine to add other bloggers in the community, but grow your network to include people in the finance industry, media, and other business related industries. Why? You are building a network. Think of LinkedIn as Facebook for your career persona. Connecting with people outside of your field gives you connections that you can reach out to when you have a question or problem that you cannot solve.

We all can't be strong in every aspect of life. Having people that you will meet and bring into your circle will help you grow your business. This is not the first step to blogging, but it is one of the next steps you will need to take to grow your blog.

Acknowledgements

I'M THANKFUL TO PAUL FOR giving me such a wonderful co-author experience. People can tell you that it's a lonely world of writing, and it's a testament to his joyful nature this book came together so well and with so much fun. He has done a wonderful job at being the best 'other writer' I could have.

I'm thankful to Annabella and Amanda for keeping the websites in great shape while I simply lived in the dark hole of my office and wrote this book. Without both ladies to help out with posting blogs and keeping me sane, this book would not be so great. Thank you also for the continual rounds of hot chocolate.

I'm thankful to my editor, Jane, who took a piece of writing that was good, and made it great. I can't begin to express how much I learn when she's around. She is always willing to rip my writing apart and then offer chocolate to make it all better.

I'm thankful to Rebecca for this experience. I'm glad that I have a use for my knowledge of and experience with tech products. I'm very lucky to have such an understanding person read my work and then post it for the world to see. She has guided me to becoming the writer that I am today, and she has also given me the opportunity to share my knowledge and journey into the blog world by way of this book.

I'm thankful to Amanda for all the hard work she does in making sure that people see the posts that I write, without her my social media would be dying. As a friend, she keeps me grounded and I am thankful I can count on her for support. She is my re-tweet queen and I can't wait for more exciting events that she has planned for this year.

I'm thankful to the ever calculating Annabella for her drive to make sure we are all living up to our potential, while letting us do our thing with our writing. She is the face of the book reviews but also a great teacher, for me while I learned the blogging ropes. I owe a lot of my ability to my job well to her. I also use her as a sounding board. Thank you for always listening. She even puts the calculator down when I'm speaking. It's a marvel. Either a book or a calculator in her hands.

But most importantly I'm thankful to all of our readers and fans. Without all of you, I wouldn't be able to keep posting. Your comments are always positive and supportive. I know that in the blogging world, if readers don't like something about your blog, they will let you know. I work hard every day to make sure each one of my posts is of the best quality that I can put out. I respect all the suggestions that readers give me, and I strive to make every post worth your precious time.

We are both thankful for our family and friends. You have all encouraged us to work harder and be better in our writing and our lives.

GLOSSARY OF BLOGGING TERMS

App: Found on smartphones, also known as application software. This is also known as a web app, or a mobile app. All of these are designed to help a person use the computer or the Internet better. These are simply computer programs.

Archived: How several blog posts are saved on a website in one place. A reader can go back through a blog by using a series of dates and read the posts this way, but it is slow and not used as often.

Blog: The shortened, and most common term for 'web log'. It is also used by many writers as a verb for the online version of writing. "I blog about cooking" or "I blog about writing."

Blog Formatted: The way a blog should look to a reader. There aren't set rules, but in general a blog will look different based on the topic you are writing about.

Bloggers: What a writer is known as in the blog community. A blogger is anyone who writes a blog, even if it is not about writing.

Blogosphere: How the many blogs in the world are termed as. Originally, this was a joke made by Brad Graham, but caught on. It means the way blogs are interconnected with one another.

CEO: Chief Executive Officer. In a business this is the most visible and highest ranking person in the company.

CFO: Chief Financial Officer. In a business this person reports to the CEO, and is in charge of the business's finance. For smaller companies, a CFO can also do day to day tasks, but this people will have a background in finances and accounting.

COO: Chief Operating Officer. This person is in charge of the day to day dealings of a business. On a blog, they would be the ones who make sure team meetings are held, and emails are sent and everyone knows and understands their duties.

Downloading: This is the act of moving or copying data from one place to another. It is normally in reference to loading information or files from the Internet to another place, such as a computer hard drive.

Editing: This is the process of selecting and preparing any type of writing used to convey information. The editing process can involve correction, condensation, organization, and many other modifications performed with an intention of producing a correct, consistent, accurate and complete work. The editing process often begins with one person- the blogger, continuing as a collaboration between an editor and blogger as the work is created. This is a long term process which will allow for all parties to learn about better communication.

Facebook: One of the major social networking sites in the world. Most writers will have a page on Facebook for passing information to their readers and for getting people to come and read their blogs.

Format: How a blog, or a book is arranged. When a writer talks about format they are referring to how people will put together a book or a blog post based on what is normally displayed.

Google+: A social networking site owned by parent company Google. It is widely used by bloggers and others alike, who 'share' and 'plus' the pages they enjoy. A plus on Google is the same as a like on Facebook.

Link: A link in the computing world is short for 'hyperlink' which is the way a computer learns a person needs to move to another part of the Internet. Normally, this link is underlined so people know to click on their mouse to go to the appropriate page.

LinkedIn: A professional social media site. This is where professionals make connections between each other.

Media Promo: This is short for media promotion. In this a person is getting coverage about a blog or a writer. The more people see you, the better the chance that your blog will grow. A means of media promotion is using Twitter or Facebook.

Network: A network is a group of people who you know, or people a person you know, knows.

President: Similar to the CEO, a president is the head of the company. They deal with growth and vision but are often linked with the title of CEO.

Retweet: What a person on twitter does for another follower or person on twitter. Similar to a share in Facebook. The more retweets a tweet gets from others, the more likely this tweet is popular or important.

Search Engine: A search engine is a topic on many bloggers minds. Google, Yahoo, and Bing are the three largest search engines. A person types a sentence or a few words, called search terms, and these engines look for a close match. A blogger wants to get on these to be found.

Social Media: Anything where you interact with your readers. This includes blogs.

Spam: This is normally found in the comment section, and it is a method where the person is trying to either get links to their blogs, or are trying to overload the system your website or blog is on. Most spam is obvious "see my site" and some of it isn't. This is usually unwanted, and there is a lot from one source.

Template: a pre-set outline or view for a blog or website, used so that the format does not have to be recreated each time it is used. These are generally free, and a good starting point for most bloggers.

Traffic: The technical terms for a reader. When a person says I get traffic on my blog, they mean they are getting readers. Traffic is also where a person gets their readers from. Readers can find a blog using the search engines, such as Google, Bing or Yahoo, and also with the social networking sites where a blog writer has their blogs listed.

Twitter: Another social networking site. This particular site is based on the idea people share information with each other using 140 characters or less. This is one of the places to beginning with some media promotion to get readers to your blog.

URL: The short form for Universal Resource Locator. Each blog and website have a unique URL. This is also known as "web address."

Viral: This is when a blog post, or an image or a video from a blog goes through the Internet at a fast pace in a short time. This is helped when the blog posts 'links' to their site on social media sites such as Google Plus, Facebook, and Twitter.

Vlog: The short form for 'video blog' this is where the blog is not in printed form but it is in a video format. Some of the more known volggers are the 'volgbrothers' one of whom is John Green, writer of *The Fault in Our Stars* and *Paper Towns.*

About the Authors

Rebecca A Emrich is the head writer at Living a Life of Writing, and CEO of Living a Life. She loves to write, to blog and to read. She's a fairly normal person except for her obsession with hot chocolate and reading more teen novels than she should. She is the author of another non-fiction book, *In Search of the Lost Ones*, a book about the Second World War. She lives with her family in southern Ontario.

Paul Nieder is the head writer at Living a Life of Gaming, and the tech writer for Living a Life of Writing. He is also President of Living a Life. When he doesn't have tech product in his hands, he enjoys writing and blogging. He plans to host a new YouTube vlog on gaming and writing soon. He lives with his family in Southern Ontario.

Index

www.ingramcontent.com/pod-product-compliance
Lightning Source LLC
Chambersburg PA
CBHW060529030426
42337CB00021B/4193